Benjamin
Franklin

Other titles in the Inventors and Creators series include:

Dr. Seuss
Henry Ford
Jim Henson
Jonas Salk
Thomas Edison

Inventors and Creators

Benjamin Franklin

P.M. Boekhoff and Stuart A. Kallen

KIDHAVEN PRESS

THOMSON
GALE

Detroit • New York • San Diego • San Francisco
Boston • New Haven, Conn. • Waterville, Maine
London • Munich

On Cover: Benjamin Franklin.

Library of Congress Cataloging-in-Publication Data

Boekhoff, P.M. (Patti Marlene), 1957–
   Benjamin Franklin / by P.M. Boekhoff and Stuart A. Kallen.
      p. cm. — (Inventors and creators)
   Includes bibliographical references and index.
   Summary: Discusses the life of Benjamin Franklin from his
childhood until his death including his accomplishments as a printer,
scientist, statesman, and diplomat.
   ISBN 0-7377-0995-2 (hardback : alk. paper)
   1. Franklin, Benjamin, 1706–1790—Juvenile literature. 2. Statesmen—
United States—Biography—Juvenile literature. 3. Inventors—United
States—Biography—Juvenile literature. 4. Scientists—United States—
Biography—Juvenile literature. 5. Printers—United States—Biography—
Juvenile literature. [1. Franklin, Benjamin, 1706–1790. 2. Statesmen.
3. Inventors. 4. Scientists. 5. Printers.] I. Kallen, Stuart A., 1955– II. Title.
III. Series.
   E302.6.F8 B64 2002
   973.3'092—dc21

2001005078

Copyright 2002 by KidHaven Press,
an imprint of The Gale Group
10911 Technology Place, San Diego, California 92127

Printed in the U.S.A.

Contents

Founding Father

Benjamin Franklin was a founding father of the United States and a man of many talents. He was a printer and an author as well as a diplomat, politician, philosopher, inventor, and scientist. Franklin was also a **genius** and a man of great moral character. He was almost completely self-educated, and he always remained curious about various subjects throughout his life. He taught himself to write clearly and simply, and he used this mastery of proper English as a tool for improving himself, his social position, and his country.

When Franklin was born, the United States of America did not yet exist. There were thirteen colonies along the East Coast, but most of America was inhabited by Native Americans. The colonies were ruled by Great Britain, a country located thousands of miles from American shores across the Atlantic Ocean.

During Franklin's life, the United States of America was created from the thirteen colonies. During every step of that process, Franklin played a central role in helping create the country that became a symbol of

Benjamin Franklin was a man of many talents. He played an important role in the founding of the United States.

democracy in the world. As a statesman representing his country, Franklin was well known in Europe. And he used his great communication skills to represent the interests of the common people.

Franklin's democratic ideals led the way to American independence. He worked tirelessly for the common good of the American people while they were under England's rule, then for the cause of the American Revolution, and finally for the newly formed federal government that followed.

Chapter One

Printer

Benjamin Franklin was born on January 6, 1706, in Boston, Massachusetts. Benjamin's father, Josiah Franklin, was a candlemaker. Benjamin's mother, Abiah Folger, was Josiah's second wife. Ben was the fifteenth of seventeen children, but he was a special child. He was curious and inventive and taught himself to read when he was very young.

Young Ben liked to fly kites, swim, canoe, and fish in Boston Harbor. Ben loved the water and wanted to be a sailor when he grew up, but Ben's father wanted Ben to be a minister. In his autobiography, Ben Franklin remembered learning from the conversations of his father:

> I remember well his being frequently visited by leading people, who consulted him for his opinion in affairs of the town or of the church he belonged to, and showed a great deal of respect for his judgment and advice; he was also much consulted by private persons about their affairs when any difficulty occurred.[1]

An artist's illustration of Benjamin Franklin's birthplace.

Josiah could afford to send Ben to school for only two years, from age eight to ten. After that, Benjamin worked in his father's business, making candles and soap. Benjamin liked to read at night by candlelight, but he did not like working in his father's shop. Because Ben loved books, his father suggested that Ben should become a printer.

Benjamin and His Brother

When Ben was twelve, his father sent Ben to work for James, Ben's half brother who had just come back from England with a new printing press. Benjamin learned the printing trade from James. In Ben's spare time, he educated himself. He took notes as he read books, then tried to write from memory what he had just learned. Later he would compare his writing to the original to see how well he remembered it.

In 1721 James started the *New England Courant*, the second newspaper ever published in America. At the age of fifteen, Benjamin ran the printing press and delivered the newspaper every day. He also wanted to write for the paper, but he did not think James would let him. Instead, Benjamin secretly wrote letters to the paper and slid them under the door. He signed them Mrs. Silence Dogood.

Young Ben Franklin runs the printing press at the *New England Courant.*

James and the other writers thought Silence was funny and wise. James published the letters, not knowing that Silence Dogood was Benjamin. The people of Boston, Massachusetts, loved the stories and poems of Mrs. Silence Dogood. Young Benjamin's early concern with serious political issues was revealed in a Dogood letter printed when he was sixteen years old, quoted in *The Real Benjamin Franklin:* "Without freedom of thought there can be no such thing as wisdom, and no such thing as public liberty without free speech, which is the right of every man as [long as] he does not hurt or control the right of another. . . . Only the wicked governors of men dread what is said of them."[2]

Against Tyranny

As an American colony of England at that time, Massachusetts was ruled by the British king and his colonial authorities. Like many of the colonists, Benjamin and James were born of parents who had come from England. But the *New England Courant* often published stories that displeased the colonial government. As a result, in 1722 James Franklin was imprisoned for a month. After he was released, the authorities ruled that James would no longer be allowed to print the paper.

To get around this ruling, James published the *New England Courant* under Benjamin's name, but James secretly remained in control. With this new situation, however, Benjamin was the one who would go to jail if the authorities were displeased. Because of this, Benjamin began to fight with James over the contents of the paper.

Sometimes when they argued, James beat Benjamin for questioning his authority. In his autobiography, Franklin wrote, "I [believe] his harsh and tyrannical treatment of me . . . [impressed] me with that **aversion** to **arbitrary** power that has stuck to me my whole life."[3]

On His Own

Because of disagreements with James, when Benjamin was seventeen years old he sold some of his books and ran away. He arrived in Philadelphia, Pennsylvania, in October 1723, friendless, penniless, hungry, and tired. Ben learned very early how to make many friends, however. Using his good manners, intelligence, charm, and cheerfulness, he soon found work in Samuel Keimer's print shop and made many new friends.

One new friend was Sir William Keith, the royal governor of the colony of Pennsylvania. Sir Keith offered to pay for Franklin to go to London to finish his training as a printer and to buy the equipment needed to start his own print shop in Philadelphia. Franklin thought this was a good idea, and he went to London in December 1724. But Sir Keith did not send the money he had promised.

Once again, Franklin found himself without money or friends in a strange city. To support himself, he quickly found work at Palmer's, one of the best printing houses in London. Later he worked at another respected shop called Watt's. Printing methods at these businesses were far more advanced than those in America. Soon the talented young man became a master printer. He worked

Franklin, pictured here at age twenty, ran away from home at seventeen.

hard and saved his money so he could return home to America.

Benjamin Franklin, Printer

In October 1726, Franklin returned to Philadelphia and continued to work as a printer. In September 1729, he bought a half interest in the *Pennsylvania Gazette*, a dull, poorly edited weekly newspaper. With his witty writing style and careful selection of news, he made the paper entertaining and informative. Before long, the *Gazette* became one of the most popular papers in the colonies.

In 1730, at twenty-four years old, Franklin became the sole owner and editor of the *Gazette*. With his success he was able to marry Deborah Read and start a family. Although she could barely read when they met, Deborah learned quickly and soon helped her husband in his work. They had three children: Francis, William, and Sarah. Francis, however, died at the age of four.

Deborah Read Franklin learned to read so she could help her husband with his work.

Articles, Almanacs, and Books

The Franklins' hard work brought them wealth, and Benjamin's writings brought him fame. Franklin wrote articles encouraging people to work hard, save money, and be kind and fair. He also printed many books written by others and so became Philadelphia's first bookseller.

At that time, however, books were so expensive that only wealthy people could afford them. To make education more available to the common person, Franklin started the first public library by convincing his friends to gather a collection of their books together and make them available to the people of Philadelphia. The idea caught on, and libraries sprang up throughout the colonies.

Benjamin Franklin also published a yearly calendar called *Poor Richard's Almanack* from 1732 until 1757. It was a small, inexpensive booklet full of practical information and advice. Writing wise and witty sayings under the name Poor Richard, Franklin often

Franklin greets customers outside his Philadelphia print shop and bookstore.

discussed his philosophy of success: Work hard and save money. *Poor Richard's Almanack* told farmers the best times to plant and harvest, and it included jokes, stories, inventions, cures, and recipes. People knew this popular publication was the work of Benjamin Franklin, and it made him famous.

Chapter Two

Scientist

Franklin spent his life looking for knowledge and truth and writing about what he found. He used his writings to improve life for others, and his compassion and talent brought him wealth and fame. At the age of thirty, he entered public life, where his actions would be as helpful and wise as his words.

In 1736 Benjamin Franklin was chosen to become clerk of the Pennsylvania Assembly, a political post he then held for fifteen years. During this time, Franklin met some of the most prosperous and well-educated people in America. These contacts helped him to secure jobs printing items of public business such as legal documents, voting ballots, and paper money.

He also used this political power to help people by making Philadelphia a better place to live. He organized the city's volunteer fire department into a paid fire company, and he reformed the city police department. He found better methods to pave, clean, and light the streets. He used his newspapers to rally support for these and other public projects, such as building a hospital for the poor.

Franklin used his knowledge and writings to help others.

In 1737 he was appointed deputy postmaster of Philadelphia. He then served at this post for forty years, eventually becoming the top postmaster in the country. Franklin used his power to vastly improve the postal service for the colonies.

Inventor

Franklin saw another problem in Philadelphia that needed to be solved. Smoke from fireplaces used to heat buildings made the sky smoky and sooty. Sparks that flew out of the chimneys sometimes set the wooden houses on fire.

Inside the houses, people gathered around their fireplaces because most of the heat went up the chimney, so the rooms often were cold. Franklin solved these problems by inventing a cast-iron stove that heated the entire room while using much less firewood than a fireplace.

Franklin printed a pamphlet to explain how the stoves were made, how to use them, and what their advantages were over other heating methods. After seeing the pamphlet, the governor of Pennsylvania offered to give Franklin a **patent** on the stove. A patent would allow Franklin to make money on every stove made. Though the patent would be worth a fortune, Franklin gave his invention as freely as he had given his other ideas. In his pamphlet, reprinted in his autobiography, he gave the reason: "That, as we enjoy great advantages from the inventions of others, we should be glad of an opportunity to serve others by an invention of ours; and this we should do freely and generously."[4]

Studying Science

Franklin continued to learn and expand his ideas. He taught himself to read French, German, Italian, Latin, and Spanish. With these skills, he read the best works of European scientists, which at that time were considered

The cast-iron stove was just one of Franklin's many ideas.

a form of **philosophy**. He began to write letters to other American scientists and in 1743, he started the American Philosophical Society so scientists could meet to talk about new ideas, experiments, and scientific viewpoints.

Shortly after starting the scientific group, Franklin decided to retire and devote the rest of his life to science. In a letter to a friend, published in *The Real Benjamin Franklin,* he expressed his happiness at retirement:

> [I will have] no other tasks than such as I shall . . . give myself, . . . enjoying what I look upon as a great happiness: leisure to read, study, make experiments, and converse at large with such ingenious and worthy men as are pleased to honor me with their friendship of acquaintance, on such

The American Philosophical Society still operates today in this building in Pennsylvania.

points as may produce something for the common benefit of mankind, uninterrupted by the little cares and fatigues of business.[5]

Lightning in a Jar

Of all his scientific studies, the study of electricity held the most interest for Franklin. In 1747 he began his electrical experiments and proved that lightning is a kind of electricity. He reported his experiments in letters to fellow scientists in England. Franklin became a well-known scientist in England and France and exchanged letters with other leading scientists.

Franklin believed that lightning, like other electricity, could be attracted by a pointed metal rod. In 1752 he attached a lightning rod to a silk kite and tied a silk ribbon and an iron key to the end of the kite string. Then, he went out with his son William to fly the kite during a thunderstorm.

Luckily for Franklin, lightning did not directly strike the rod. Such a hit by a lightning bolt probably would have killed him, as it did others who tried this dangerous experiment. The pointed rod on Franklin's kite attracted some of the electricity from a nearby lightning bolt and the electricity traveled through the wet kite string and into the iron key. From the key, the electricity traveled into a Leyden jar—a battery used to collect and store electricity. The jar captured and held electricity. With this experiment Franklin trapped lightning in a jar.

Franklin flies a kite in his experiment with lightning.

A lightning rod is attached to the chimney of a house.

Franklin knew that when lightning struck a building, it often burned down. His lightning rod, when attached to the top of a building, could catch the lightning and conduct it into the ground where it would do no harm. As always, Franklin shared his ideas freely to help others. In the 1753 *Poor Richard's Almanack,* he published simple instructions for his readers to make their own lightning rods.

Inventions for Readers

Some of Franklin's practical inventions were helpful for one of his favorite activities, reading. For instance, he invented bifocals—eyeglasses used to see both near and far.

To make bifocals, he cut two pairs of glasses in half, each with a different type of lens. One pair was used for reading and seeing close-up, and the other for seeing far away. Franklin put the two types of lenses together, the lower half for reading, the upper half for seeing distances. Later, whenever Franklin spoke in public, reading his speeches from printed pages, his bifocals allowed him to see his audience as he spoke to them.

Franklin invented bifocals to help people see better both near and far.

Franklin also invented chairs that made reading more pleasant. One of his chairs had a desk attached to hold books. Another is the rocking chair. Franklin attached rounded pieces of wood to his chair to create this relaxing seat. He also invented a chair that turned into a ladder so he could get books down from high shelves. For books that were on really high shelves, he invented a pole that could grasp things from far away.

The creative Franklin invented many items and shared his plans freely because he felt that a person's highest duty is to serve others with good works. He never accepted money for his discoveries and inventions, saying his ideas belonged to everyone. He wrote about them in newspapers, pamphlets, letters, and scientific papers, and he shared them in his almanac.

Chapter Three

Statesman

As Philadelphia's postmaster, Benjamin Franklin made improvements in communication that helped to unite the colonies. His actions brought great men together to solve problems and help create a better society. In 1751, while he was working on his electrical experiments, Franklin was elected to represent Philadelphia at the Pennsylvania Assembly. As a representative of the people, Franklin began to act on the idea of uniting the colonies to form a single American nation.

The English and French governments both wanted to control the colonies and the land to the west of the colonies. Franklin wanted the colonies to join together to defend themselves against the French and France's Indian allies. In 1754 he published America's first political cartoon. Its caption, "JOIN, OR DIE,"[6] reflected this tense situation.

Later that year, the conflict sparked the French and Indian War, pitting French soldiers and their Native American allies against the English. Caught between the two warring countries were the Six Nations of the

JOIN, or DIE.

In America's first political cartoon, Franklin illustrates his belief that the colonies should unite.

Iroquois, a group of Native American tribes who sided with the English.

As the war began, the British sent representatives from seven colonies to meet in Albany, New York, to make a treaty of alliance with the Six Nations. Franklin represented Pennsylvania at the meeting, known as the Albany Congress.

While working out the treaty Franklin drew up the Albany Plan of Union, a program to unite the colonies under one democratic government. His plan would allow the colonies to defend themselves so they would not need English protection, taxation, or rule. It would take thirty-three years, however, before Franklin's idea would help to shape the U.S. Constitution in 1787.

The French and Indian War

Meanwhile, the British government decided to send troops to fight the French and Indians, and tax the colonists for the cost. In his autobiography, Franklin wrote: "The British government, not [choosing] to permit the union of the colonies as propos'd at Albany, and to trust that union with their defense, lest they should thereby grow too military, and feel their own strength . . . sent over General Braddock with two regiments of regular English troops for that purpose."[7]

When Braddock arrived, Franklin met with him and assured him that the assembly was prepared to do everything it could to help him fight the French. Braddock was having trouble finding enough wagons

The British sent General Braddock and two regiments to fight the French and the Indians.

and supplies and was ready to give up. Franklin helped him by making agreements with Pennsylvania farmers for the use of their supplies, horses, and wagons. Franklin also promised to repay the farmers for anything captured or destroyed in the war, and he made good on that promise.

Taxation Without Representation

Franklin had once again shown himself to be resourceful and fair. Colonists and outsiders alike knew him to be a man who kept his word. These same qualities made him an able spokesman for the farmers in their fight against wealthy landholders. The farmers were angry that they had to pay extra taxes to fund the war while large landholders did not. Franklin traveled to England to argue the farmers' cause, and won.

While he was in England, Franklin tried to win sympathy for American liberty and freedom from English rule. He made friends with scientists, philosophers, historians, and politicians. He not only won sympathy for American ideas, but also the respect of many leading people in England.

Franklin returned to Philadelphia in 1762, and the English won the French and Indian War the next year. In 1764 Franklin returned to England to petition the king for a new colonial government. But the king claimed he needed more American tax money to pay for the French and Indian War. In 1765 the British governing body known as **Parliament** passed the Stamp Act, which required all colonists to buy stamps and put them on all printed materials, such as newspapers, almanacs, legal papers, and even playing cards.

Franklin was in England when the Stamp Act was passed, and he protested it by writing funny essays against it for London newspapers. Across the ocean, colonists were angered by the Stamp Act, saying that taxation without representation in Parliament was **tyranny**. Violent protests erupted and people wanted to form their own governments to raise tax money and control how it was spent.

Fortifying Character

Because Franklin was in England, he did not know how strongly the colonists opposed the Stamp Act. He counseled them to accept it, which made him unpopular at

The Stamp Act required that colonists buy and place stamps like these on all printed materials.

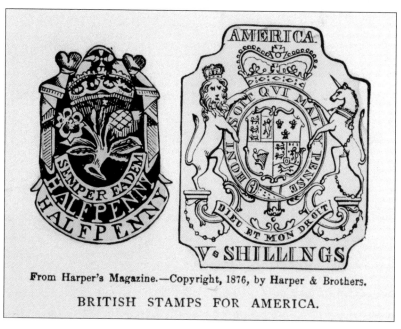

From Harper's Magazine.—Copyright, 1876, by Harper & Brothers.

BRITISH STAMPS FOR AMERICA.

American colonists react angrily to the passage of the Stamp Act.

home. Some of his enemies tried to blame him for the passage of the Stamp Act, although he had done his best to prevent it. His sister, Jane Mecom, wrote a letter to him, stating how it made her sad that he was treated so unfairly. His reply, in a personal letter published in *Mr. Franklin*, expresses his positive attitude:

> As to the Abuses I meet with . . . you must know I number them among my Honors. One cannot behave so as to obtain the Esteem of the Wise and Good, without drawing on one's self at the same time the Envy and Malice of the Foolish and Wicked. . . . The best Men have always had their Share of this Treatment. . . . A Man therefore has reason to be asham'd of himself when he meets with none of it. . . . [Such] enemies do a Man some good, while they think they are doing him harm, by fortifying the Character they would destroy.[8]

In 1766 Franklin was questioned in the British House of Commons about the effects of the Stamp Act on the colonies. His testimony influenced England to repeal the act.

The American Revolution Begins

Soon after the repeal, however, new plans for taxing the colonies were introduced in Parliament, and Franklin knew that it would lead to war. To protest the new tax on tea, American Patriots dumped hundreds of chests of tea into Boston Harbor. In England, Franklin fought

Colonists dump tea into Boston Harbor in an event that became known as the Boston Tea Party.

against the tyranny of royal governors who ruled the colonies. As a result, Franklin became unpopular with the English and the king took away Franklin's job as postmaster general of the colonies.

Meanwhile, Franklin experienced great grief upon hearing that his wife Deborah died in Philadelphia while he was far away. Franklin sailed for America after eleven years abroad and reached Philadelphia on May 5, 1775. When he arrived, the American Revolution had already started. The first shots of the war were fired in Massachusetts at Lexington and Concord on April 19.

The Declaration of Independence

When he arrived, Franklin learned that his son William had vowed loyalty to England's king. William had once worked side by side with his father for the American cause. Now, however, he worked for the king as royal governor of New Jersey. Father and son parted ways.

Franklin set to work on behalf of the revolutionary government. He took a position as postmaster, and he donated his salary to help soldiers wounded in the war. He was also chosen to be a member of the Second Continental Congress, which was formed to govern the colonies. At sixty-nine, he was the oldest member.

Franklin served on a committee of five men chosen to draft the Declaration of Independence. Although

Franklin (left) was one of five men chosen to write the Declaration of Independence.

Thomas Jefferson did most of the writing, he asked Franklin and John Adams to make corrections before sending it to Congress. The draft was approved on July 4, 1776.

The Declaration of Independence told the world why the American Revolution was needed. It stated that the government's purpose was to guarantee the rights of its citizens. If the government takes away those rights, it is up to the citizens to revolt against the tyranny of that government. Protests and patience had not given the American colonists these rights, so they declared their independence from their government. After several decades of helping Americans move toward independence, Franklin was about to see his dream become reality.

Chapter Four

Diplomat

In 1776 Benjamin Franklin went to France to ask the king to help the Americans fight the British. Though seventy years old, and in poor health, Franklin charmed the French. He had become well known in France during earlier visits as a man of great intelligence and wit. His honesty, fairness, humor, and gracious manner made him extremely popular in both political and artistic circles.

Because he was so loved, Franklin was very helpful to the American colonies in their fight for equality and freedom. Franklin knew how to speak to the concerns of powerful people. When he met with French rulers, he told them that if France's British enemies won the war, Britain would have more power over France. To the businesspeople, Franklin spoke of the advantage of trading directly with the colonists, without the cost of British taxes added to the goods.

Philosophers and artists spoke with Franklin about forming a more enlightened society. To them, he represented the freedom and liberty of a new world. Some of

Franklin charms King Louis XVI and his court.

the French believed in those ideals, and they would one day have their own revolution. In addition, other people throughout Europe began to long for American ideals of freedom. In a letter written in 1777 to his friend Samuel Cooper, printed in *The Life and Letters of Benjamin Franklin,* Franklin wrote:

> All Europe is on our side. . . . Those who live un-der arbitrary power do nevertheless approve of lib-erty, and wish for it. . . . They read . . . our separate colony **constitutions** with rapture; and there are such numbers everywhere, who talk of [moving] to America, with their families and fortunes, as soon as peace and our independence shall be es-tablished. . . . Hence it is a common observation here, that our cause is *the cause of all mankind,* and

that we are fighting for their liberty in defending our own.[9]

On February 6, 1778, Franklin negotiated a treaty of alliance with France, which became the turning point of the American Revolution. Then, against the powerful opposition of the French minister of finance, Franklin did what perhaps no other man could have done. He managed to secure liberal grants, loans, and supplies from King Louis XVI of France. Although Louis XVI was already bankrupt, he was willing to go further into debt to help the United States win its independence from France's old enemies, the British.

Franklin (seated, left) negotiates a treaty of alliance with French officials.

War and Peace

In America, members of the Colonial Army, led by George Washington, were thankful for the money that would keep them fed, clothed, and armed during the revolution. In France, Franklin secured loans, bought and sent supplies, exchanged prisoners of war, gathered information, and recruited French soldiers to serve in the army and navy in America. He encouraged American and French pirates to raid British ships and send the goods to the American colonies.

In 1781 the British surrendered and the war ended. Without Franklin's help, the American Revolution would not have succeeded. After the war, Franklin was the first to begin peace talks with British representatives who went to Paris. They agreed on the basic points of the peace treaty, but they had to wait for American representatives John Jay and John Adams to arrive to make the treaty final.

Finally, the Treaty of Paris was signed on September 3, 1783. The treaty promised complete independence for the new American nation and defined its borders. In a letter printed in *The Life and Letters of Benjamin Franklin*, Franklin wrote, "We are now friends with England and with all mankind. May we never see another war, for in my opinion *there never was a good war or a bad peace*."[10]

In March 1785, Franklin returned to Philadelphia, where he was treated as a hero. When he arrived he was met by a huge crowd of people who held a parade in his honor. Throughout Philadelphia churches rang their

General George Washington and his men defeated the British with Benjamin Franklin's help.

bells and dignitaries gave speeches and held celebrations. Franklin was reunited with his daughter Sarah and his grandchildren, and he was immediately chosen to be president of Pennsylvania.

Framer of the U.S. Constitution

At the time Franklin returned to Philadelphia there was no president of the United States. The states were not yet united under one government. Instead, they were a **confederation** of thirteen state governments. Lawyers, bankers, and wealthy landowners decided that the new country needed a strong central government, a central bank, and a new constitution. They pressed for a Constitutional Convention and in 1787, Franklin was elected a delegate to the convention to draw up a new constitution.

Franklin speaks at the Constitutional Convention in 1787.

Benjamin Franklin put his whole heart into the work. He attended the meetings faithfully and lent his wisdom to the arguments. His humor and sense of fairness helped the delegates work together to find compromises. Although he did not agree with everything in the U.S. Constitution, Franklin worked to get it adopted.

Even when he was very old, Franklin's ideas were ahead of his time. He believed in liberty, mercy, and justice for everybody, and he wrote emotional pleas in favor of freeing the slaves. One of his last public acts was to sign a petition to the U.S. Congress, on February 12, 1790, urging the abolition of slavery. Unfortunately, slavery would not be abolished for another seventy-five years.

Two months after sending his petition, on April 17, 1790, Franklin died at home. He was eighty-four years old.

Franklin did much to make the ideals of true democracy into a reality. He was humble and cared about making a government that was truly by the people, of the people, and for the people. He has been called statesman, philosopher, diplomat, and many other important titles. But he called himself a printer, and his epitaph, written when he was twenty-three years old, shows his humor and humility:

The Body of
B. Franklin,
Printer;
Like the Cover of an old Book,
Its Contents torn out,
And Stript of its Lettering and Gilding,
Lies here, Food for Worms.
But the Work shall not be wholly lost;
For it will, as he believed, appear once more,
In a new and more perfect Edition,
Corrected and amended
By the Author.
He was born Jan. 6, 1706.
Died 17– [11]

Notes

Chapter 1: Printer

1. Benjamin Franklin, *The Autobiography of Benjamin Franklin*. Garden City, NY: Houghton Mifflin, 1923, p. 30.
2. Quoted in Andrew M. Allison, *The Real Benjamin Franklin*. Washington, DC: National Center for Constitutional Studies, 1987, p. 14.
3. Franklin, *The Autobiography of Benjamin Franklin*, p. 42.

Chapter 2: Scientist

4. Franklin, *The Autobiography of Benjamin Franklin*, p. 165.
5. Quoted in Allison, *The Real Benjamin Franklin*, p. 76.

Chapter 3: Statesman

6. Quoted in Allison, *The Real Benjamin Franklin*, p. 97.
7. Franklin, *The Autobiography of Benjamin Franklin*, p. 188.
8. Leonard W. Labaree and Whitfield J. Bell Jr., eds., *Mr. Franklin: A Selection from His Personal Letters*. New Haven, CT: Yale University Press, 1956, p. 16.

Chapter 4: Diplomat

9. Benjamin Franklin, *The Life and Letters of Benjamin Franklin*, Eau Clare, WI: E.M. Hale, p. 258.
10. Franklin, *The Life and Letters of Benjamin Franklin*, p. 305.
11. Quoted in the Editors of Country Beautiful, *The Most Amazing American: Benjamin Franklin*. Wakesha, WI: Country Beautiful, 1973, p. 157.

Glossary

arbitrary: Determined by chance or whim rather than by reason, law, moral standards, or basic truth.

aversion: Intense dislike and avoidance.

confederation: A group of states or nations who are friends or allies.

constitution: The system of basic laws that govern the government.

genius: Having a great deal of intelligence.

Parliament: The lawmaking body of Great Britain and other countries.

patent: A government grant giving an inventor the right to be the only one to make, use, and sell an invention for a period of time.

philosophy: Love of wisdom or knowledge; applying human ideas to the study of nature.

tyranny: Having total power, especially when it is used unjustly or cruelly.

For Further Exploration

David A. Adler, *Benjamin Franklin: Printer, Inventor, Statesman.* New York: Holiday House, 1992. A biography of Benjamin Franklin, illustrated by Lyle Miller.

Aliki Brandenburg, *The Many Lives of Benjamin Franklin.* New York: Simon & Schuster, 1977, 1988. A short, illustrated biography that explains Benjamin Franklin's activities and achievements.

Jean Fritz, *What's the Big Idea, Ben Franklin?* New York: Coward, McCann, & Geoghegan, 1976. A short biography of Benjamin Franklin, a printer, inventor, and statesman who influenced the early history of America. Illustrated by Margot Tomes.

Steve Parker, *Benjamin Franklin and Electricity.* New York: Chelsea House, 1995. Describes the discoveries of Benjamin Franklin, scientist and inventor.

Robert Quackenbush, *Benjamin Franklin and His Friends.* New York: Pippin Press, 1991. The life of Benjamin Franklin is described through the many kinds of friendships that influenced him. Illustrated with cartoons.

Index

Picture Credits

About the Authors

Patti Marlene Boekhoff has cocreated a dozen books for young readers about art, ecology, states, and Native Americans, and she has illustrated many book covers. In addition, Ms. Boekhoff creates theatrical scenic works and other large paintings. In her spare time, she writes poetry and fiction, studies herbal medicine, and tends her garden.

Stuart A. Kallen is the author of more than 150 nonfiction books for children and young adults. He has written extensively about Native Americans and American history. In addition, Mr. Kallen has written award-winning children's videos and television scripts. In his spare time, he is a singer/songwriter/guitarist in San Diego, California.